# Composing Matters

Return
will

Patrick Allen

D1556013

UNIVERSITY OF
LIBRARY
SERVICES
CENTRAL ENGLAND

## Heinemann

*The author dedicates the pack to the students of Ifield Community College*

Heinemann Educational Publishers
Halley Court, Jordan Hill, Oxford OX2 8EJ

Part of Harcourt Limited

Heinemann is the registered trademark of Harcourt Education Limited

First published in 2002

05 04
10 9 8 7 6 5 4 3

**British Library Cataloguing in Publication Data**
A catalogue record for this book is available from the British Library

ISBN 0 435 81182 7

Typeset by Artistix, Thame, Oxon
Printed and bound in Spain by Edelvives

**Acknowledgements**
The author would like to thank the following for their help and support during the preparation of the course: Jamie Harrison, Jade Carrington, Daniel Jackson, Daniel Schofield, Liz Harrison, Margaret Vodden, Angeline Bell, Claire Lewis, Anne and Alun Lewis, Sue Walton, Liz Tyler, Kate Webster and the team at Heinemann.

The publishers would like to thank the following for permission to use photographs:
AKG/Uffizi Gallery, p. 35 (top right); Empics, p. 34; Glasgow Science Centre/Keith Hunter, p. 35 (bottom); Hutchison/Robert Francis, p. 14 (bottom); Panos Pictures, p. 14 (top); Photodisc, p. 35 (top left); Tate Gallery, London, p. 35 (middle right).

Cover photograph by Getty One

The publishers would like to thank the following for use of films:
© Jamie Harrison. Filmed with the help of Daniel Jackson, Jade Carrington and Daniel Schofield.

The publishers have made every effort to contact copyright holders. However, if any material has been incorrectly acknowledged, the publishers would be pleased to correct this at the earliest opportunity.

Tel: 01865 888058  www.heinemann.co.uk

# Contents

# Introduction

Welcome to *Composing Matters*. This book is written alongside a Teacher's Resource Pack and a CD-ROM, which provides musical backings to help you compose, as well as recordings of compositions.

This book contains twenty-five projects which aim to:

- provide inspiration for original compositions
- develop your improvising and composing skills
- broaden your musical knowledge
- develop your performing and listening skills
- give you opportunities to work on your own
- give opportunities to work with others
- provide enjoyment.

## What is composing?

Composing takes place when someone invents music themselves. Usually it will be based on ideas or styles which already exist.

## What is improvising?

Improvising takes place when you make up music as you go along. Usually there are clear rules, which make improvising easier than it sounds.

## Using the projects

The projects are best done under the guidance of a teacher, who will have access to the CD-ROM and Teacher's Resource Pack. You do not need to work your way systematically through the book, but you may find the following information useful for structuring your learning.

- *Projects which develop skills*
  Projects 1 and 3 develop skills with rhythm and percussion.
  Projects 2, 4 and 9 develop skills in melody writing.
  Projects 17, 18 and 20 develop skills in composing with **chords**.
  Projects 6, 9, 21 and 23 develop skills in structure.
  Projects 9 and 13 develop skills in setting words.

- *Projects which encourage free expression*
  Projects 5, 7, 11, 15 and 16 present material that allows you to explore and experiment freely to create compositions.

- *Projects related to film and media*
  Projects 12, 14 and 25 use film and television as starting points for composing.

- *Projects inspired by music from a variety of times and cultures*
  Projects 5, 9, 19, 22 and 24 use music from other times and cultures as a starting point for composing.

- *Projects inspired by popular music*
  Projects 3, 6, 8, 12, 14, 20, 21, 22, 23 and 25 can be strongly related to modern popular culture.

## Imitate, echo, improvise

*Composing Matters* encourages you to listen, improvise and perform as part of the composing process. Many projects begin with the same routine, where you:

- imitate and echo short examples given by the teacher, usually over a backing from the CD-ROM
- improvise freely over the backing
- begin to develop your composition at an instrument or by singing.

## Using the CD-ROM

Your teacher has the backings and examples on a CD-ROM. Normally these will be played to you at an appropriate moment in the lesson. If you would like to work with a backing on your own, they are stored as **MIDI files** which can be copied onto floppy disk and played through a **sequencer** or media player. If you are composing at a computer with sequencing software such as Cubase, Cakewalk or Logic, you can even make the MIDI file part of your composition. Some of the backings are also on the CD-ROM as audio files, and can be played on a normal CD player.

MIDI, audio and video files on the CD-ROM are highlighted throughout this book as follows.

 MIDI file

 Audio file

 Video file

## Working as a group

It is important to experience composing as part of a group, where you can share ideas and perform your composition to the class. Many projects in *Composing Matters* are suitable for group work. Always plan your work carefully and take appropriate instruments with you to your rehearsal area.

## Working alone

Some projects suit individual work. You can sing, work with an instrument, with a computer or keyboard-based sequencer, or work on paper.

## Evaluating your work

It is important that you have a sense of how you have done. Did the music fulfil your wishes or the demands of the assignment? Did the audience understand your intentions? The Teacher's Resource Pack has frameworks that can be copied to help you do this.

## References and Glossary

At the back of the book there are references and information concerning rhythm, chords, scales, musical language, instruments and music technology. There is also an atmosphere glossary, which gives you ideas and starting points for expressing moods, atmospheres and feelings.

## Research

The end of each project gives suggestions for research. This can be done from dictionaries and encyclopaedias, music reference books and from the Internet. If you use the Internet, or other computer-based resources, select your information carefully and avoid making long 'print outs'.

## Finally

I hope you enjoy the projects in *Composing Matters*, and that they will give you skills, knowledge and pleasure.

# Rhythm (1)

## UNDERSTANDING WORDS AND SYMBOLS

a)  ♩  = a crotchet, worth one beat

b)  ♫  = two quavers, each worth half a beat

c)  𝄽  = a crotchet rest (silence for one beat)

d)  ▬  = a minim rest (silence for two beats)

e)  A bar of 4/4 (adds up to four crotchets per bar)

**Unison:** all performers play the same notes

**Ostinato:** a repeated pattern or phrase

**Imitation:** repeating the phrase of another part

**Round (Canon):** exact imitation of another part

---

### Activity 1  Learning a rhythm

Learn to clap the following three-bar phrase.

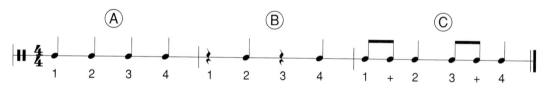

---

### Activity 2  Composing a single-bar ostinato

1  Compose a one-bar phrase in 4/4. Write it down (like the example below). Learn how to clap the phrase. When you repeat the bar it becomes an ostinato.

2  Find a partner. Practise each other's phrases. Remember to steadily count in '1, 2, 3, 4' to set the tempo before you play.

3  Now choose *one* phrase, which you will both clap as an ostinato.

4  Find another pair to work with so there are four of you. Someone should count in. After the count of 4, each pair will clap its ostinato so both ostinati are running at once.

5  Continue as instructed by your teacher.

## Activity 3  Composing a longer phrase

1   Compose a longer phrase lasting two or four bars. Write it down. Play as instructed by your teacher.

2   Find a partner and learn to play each other's rhythms. Choose *one* of them and learn to clap it together.

3   Now work with another pair. Pair A will clap the longer rhythm. Pair B will repeat the one-bar ostinato they composed for Activity 2. After counting in, both rhythms will happen at the same time. Repeat the piece as many times as you like. Try playing the piece on contrasting percussion instruments. You have performed something that looks like this:

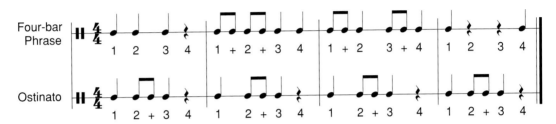

You may be asked to write your composition down in this way.

## Activity 4  Composing for two instuments

1   Compose a four-bar rhythm for two percussion instruments. The piece can include unison, imitation and independent parts. Here is an example.

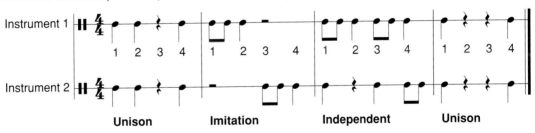

2   Perform on contrasting percussion instruments.

## Activity 5  Recording your composition

Try recording or layering any of your compositions into a computer or keyboard sequencer. If the sequencing program has a score function, see if you can print the score.

# Pentatonic melody writing

## THE PENTATONIC SCALE

A pentatonic scale uses fives notes. In Activity 1 they correspond to the black notes on a keyboard:

**C#, D#, F#, G# and A#**

In this exercise the **tonic** (key note) is D#.

### Activity 1    Imitating and improvising

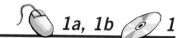

*1a, 1b*    1

1. Imitate, echo and improvise on 'black' notes over the backing, as directed by your teacher. As a musical shorthand name the notes as follows:

**C#=1, D#=2, F#=3, G#=4, A#=5**

For this activity the tonic (key) note is 2.

2. Now improvise freely and at length. You may be asked to perform your extended **improvisation** to the rest of the class.

### Activity 2    Composing answering phrases

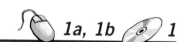

*1a, 1b*    1

1. Compose an 'answer', or balancing phrase, to complete the following melodies. Each opening will be repeated several times so you can learn it. Write down the whole phrase using numbers.

   **a)**    2     1   |   3    4    5   |

   **b)**    2    1    2   |   3    4 3   2   |

   **c)**    5    5 5   4   3   |   2    3    4   |

   **d)**    1    2    3   |   4    5    4   |

2. Now compose the opening of a **melody**, like those above. Write down your opening once you have perfected it. You can either compose the 'answer' yourself or invite another student to do so.

## Activity 3    Composing a pentatonic melody

Try to compose a short, balanced melody of four or eight bars in length. The melody needs to be memorable, and can be written down using numbers (see the example below).

… or music notation (see the example below).

## Activity 4    Composing over a pentatonic rock riff  2

The pentatonic scale in this exercise uses the 'white' notes:

**D, E, G, A, B**

The tonic is E.

1   Imitate, echo and improvise around this scale.

2   Compose short '**riffs**' over the backing using:

   **a)**   D, E, G only

   **b)**   G, A, B only

   **c)**   D, E, G, A, B.

3   Write your riffs down, then show them to another student. Try to 'layer' your riff over a partner's riff.

4   Compose a longer melody over the backing. Write it down or record it.

## Research work

1   Find out which types of music frequently use the pentatonic scale.

2   The traditional musics of which countries are most frequently associated with the pentatonic scale?

3   Find out which interval, present in the major and minor scale, is missing from the pentatonic scale.

4   Claude Debussy made frequent use of the pentatonic scale.

   **a)**   Who was he?

   **b)**   When did he live?

   **c)**   List some of his pieces that use the pentatonic scale.

5   Bring in to class an example of the pentatonic scale as used in rock or pop music.

# Rhythm (2)

## RHYTHMS

**Section A: layered ostinato**

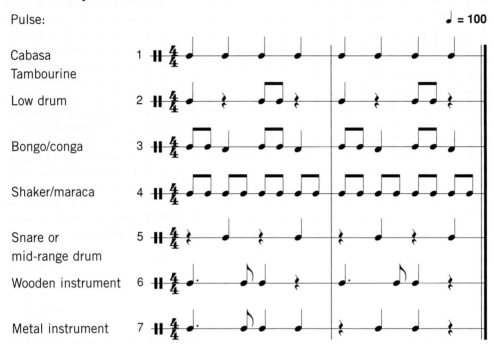

**Section B: unison rhythm**

## Activity 1 — Performing the ostinato piece

1   Learn the ostinato parts of Section A above.

2   Layer the repeating parts on top of each other.

3   Decide how many times Section A should be repeated.

4   Learn Section B. Play it twice, in unison.

5   Perform the piece using the structure A B A.

6   Now discuss what you have learned, as directed by your teacher.

## Activity 2   Composing a layered ostinato piece

1   In groups (or individually using sequencing software), compose a layered ostinato piece based on Section A (see page 10). Think about the following questions.

   a) Will all the instruments start at once, or should they enter one at a time?

   b) How will you know when to start and stop?

   c) How will you keep a steady pulse?

   d) Which instruments should play on the 'down beat'?

**TIPS**

- One instrument, possibly wooden or a tambourine, should keep the pulse.

- Make sure you have a good mixture of instruments.

- Lower pitched instruments tend to have slower rhythms. Higher pitched instruments tend to have more detail. Metal instruments stand out and can carry an important phrase.

2   Next, compose a short contrasting section.

3   Now join Sections A and B so you create a piece that follows the structure A B A. You will need to make some decisions.

   a) How many times will each section be repeated?

   b) How will you indicate when to start and when to change sections?

   c) Should all the instruments play all of the time?

4   When your piece is complete, you may be asked to perform or record it.

**TIPS**

Section B (see page 10) could contrast in any of the following ways:

- unison instead of layered
- **dynamics**
- **tempo**
- number of instruments.

## Activity 3   Writing down your composition

Write down the structure of your composition. Your teacher will guide you with this.

**Research work**

1   Find examples of compositions in any style or type of music that feature ostinato. Make a list of these.

2   Find out what 'ternary form' is. List some examples of music that use it.

# Dorian melody

## THE DORIAN MODE

The Dorian mode and the notes that form it are related to the minor scale and can have a somewhat sad quality. Much folk music from the British Isles, as well as jazz and popular music, uses this scale.

D    E    F    G    A    B    C    D

### Activity 1    Imitating and improvising

Imitate, echo and improvise in the Dorian mode over the backing, as directed by your teacher.

### Activity 2    Composing riffs in the Dorian mode

1   You are going to learn four two-bar riffs from your teacher, which you will perform with the class. Perform them in unison and in layers over the backing.

2   Compose your own two-bar riff in the Dorian mode. You can select one of the following frameworks for your riff. Remember, D is your tonic.
    a)  Using notes C, D and F. Rhythmic and lively. Middle **pitch**.
    b)  Using notes D, A and C. Slow moving. Low pitch.
    c)  Using notes D, F, G and A. Moderate pace. Middle pitch.
    d)  Using notes A, C and D. Fast and short, with long rests between playings. High pitch.

3   Perform your riff to class members. Try to combine your riff with others in the class.

### Activity 3    Composing balanced phrases

Compose a balancing phrase of two bars to complete the following four melodies. Learn to play the first two bars before you compose the rest. On which note should each melody end?

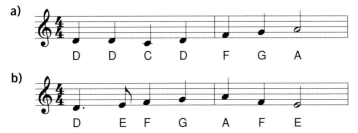

a)

D    D    C    D    F    G    A

b)

D    E    F    G    A    F    E

c)

D D   F F   G G F A

d)

D D   D F   D   E C   C

## Activity 4   Composing longer melodies

1 Compose a longer melody over the backing. Try the following four-line framework. Each line can be worth two or four bars.

- Line 1 (Phrase A) – a phrase ending on A.
- Line 2 (Phrase A1) – a similar phrase ending on D.
- Line 3 (Phrase B) – a new phrase.
- Line 4 (Phrase A1) – the same as line 2.

Here is an example.

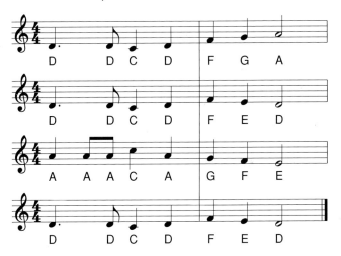

D   D C D   F G A

D   D C D   F E D

A A A C A   G F E

D   D C D   F E D

2 Perform your melody to class members and write it down using letters or notation.

## Research work

1 The Dorian mode is used in folk music, jazz, pop and early music. List any examples that you can find.

2 What is the origin of the Dorian mode? What other modes are there?

3 Find other melodies which follow the AABA structure.

# The tribe

## TRIBAL MUSIC

Music is used in all societies for social and ritual purposes. A 'social' purpose might be music to accompany work, to send a child to sleep, or to be played at a celebration or sports event. A 'ritual' purpose might be music for a religious service, for a wedding or for a ceremonial war dance. Sometimes the two purposes merge.

---

### Activity 1   Listening to ritual music  *14–17*

1 You are about to listen to some pieces of music. For each piece, try to answer the following questions.

   **a)** What voices or instruments can you hear?

   **b)** What is the mood, atmosphere or character of the piece?

   **c)** How is this atmosphere created?

   **d)** What might be the purpose of the music?

   **e)** Where in the world do you think the piece comes from?

---

### Activity 2   Setting the scene

1 You are the member of a tribe that includes your whole class. You are going to form a group to create music for the tribe.

2 There will be 'grand ceremony' for the whole tribe, at a time chosen by your teacher, for which every group must prepare music.

3 The purpose and title of your music will be one of the following.

| HUNTING | WARFARE | MAGIC |
|---|---|---|
| Music to prepare the tribe for the chase and the capture. | Music to gather strength and prepare the tribe for battle. | Music to cast a spell, change the weather or deliver a warning. |

| HEALING | LULLABY | CELEBRATION |
|---|---|---|
| Music to comfort and heal. | Music to soothe and send to sleep. | Music to celebrate a happy occasion. |

| WORK | GRIEVING |
|---|---|
| Music to keep the workers going, whether grinding corn, rowing, washing or digging. | Music to express the sadness of the community after a tragedy. |

## Activity 3 Planning your composition

1 Discuss the title you have been given, then decide the following.

   **a)** How can you use voices? For chanting, singing, speaking, whispering, shouting? Do you want to use words? Do you want to invent a language? Do you want to use dance?

   **b)** Which instruments available in your classroom would best suit your purpose? Should they be tuned or untuned? Do you need to create strong or delicate sounds? Will rhythm or melody be important?

   **c)** Will the dynamics of your piece be loud or soft? Will they change as the piece develops?

   **d)** Will the tempo of your piece be fast or slow? Will it change as the piece develops?

## Activity 4 Starting to compose

1 When you are ready, collect your instruments to develop your piece.

2 Now begin your composition. While composing, consider the following.

   **a)** Do you have the correct instruments?

   **b)** How long should the piece be?

   **c)** Does it convey the purpose of the title?

   **d)** Does the piece develop well?

   **e)** Do you need variety or contrast?

   **f)** Are all group members involved?

   **g)** How can you write down your ideas so you don't forget them?

## Activity 5 Performing your composition

1 Perform and record your piece at the grand ceremony.

2 Listen carefully to the other groups. How well did they convey the mood and purpose of their title?

# *Pitched ostinato*

## PENTATONIC AND DORIAN SCALES

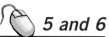 *5 and 6*

Look at the different scales below, then try the activities.

**Ostinato A: pentatonic scale**

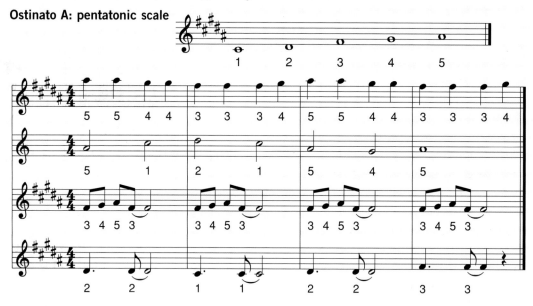

**Ostinato B: Dorian scale**

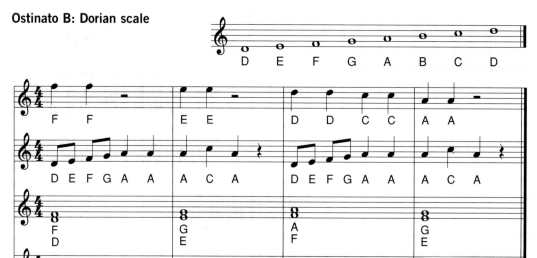

## Activity 1 — Performing the ostinati

1  Listen to one or both of the ostinati on page 16.

2  Now learn to play one of these.

## Activity 2 — Composing an ostinato piece

1  Using either of the scales on page 16, compose a layered ostinato piece. You can use any mixture of pitched instruments. Compose your pieces by first improvising short phrases. See how phrases sound against each other, then adapt them so they sound well together. You will need to work in a group (or by recording into a computer or sequencer). You will need a strong pulse.

2  Once you have composed your ostinati, decide how you will structure the piece, how it will begin and end, and whether everyone should play all of the time.

3  If you complete your ostinato (Section A), you may wish to compose a contrasting second section (Section B). This section could contrast by: texture (number of instruments or unison), tempo, dynamics, or it could be a new ostinato pattern. Structure your piece A B A.

! TIPS

- Set the pulse first, then play the lowest part followed by the others in turn.
- Learn your own part thoroughly before you perform with others.
- Decide which instruments suit each part, so you have timbres (sounds), that work well together.
- Think about how your performance will begin and end. Should you enter and exit one at a time? Will the performance need a leader/conductor?
- Think about adding/inventing new parts.

! TIPS

- Begin with the pulse, then compose your lowest part. It should be slow moving and use few notes. It can be a drone (see page 42). It must include the tonic (key note).
- The other parts should fit against each other and the pulse, but be different from each other.
- Your other parts can be faster moving.
- One other part can use longer notes.

 ## Research work

1  Find out what 'minimalism' is. Then research some examples of pieces and composers of this style. What is the connection with minimalism to this project?

2  Find examples of pitched ostinato in garage, house, hip-hop, drum 'n' bass and other modern dance styles.

# Moods and feelings

## ATMOSPHERES

### FEAR

Alone in the woods. Have I escaped? There is silence, apart from the rustle of branches in the wind. Suddenly I see the silhouette of a figure against the moonlight. For a moment I stand, frozen with fear. I start to run – faster and faster, my heart pounding, towards the small cottage. I bang on the door. The door creaks open …

### SUSPENSE

Suddenly, a sound from upstairs. Was it a floorboard creaking, or a footstep? I listen closely, but now only the ticking clock breaks the silence. A thud. I decide to investigate. Slowly and quietly I walk across the room in rhythm with the clock's tick. I enter the hallway and climb the stairs. I walk towards the bedroom door, which is slightly ajar. Slowly, gently I push it wider. A window is open and the curtains fluttering. I cast my eyes slowly around the room and move towards the window …

### DREAM

Through the soft mist, thin sunlight falls on the unicorns drinking from the silver lake. Blossom falls gently from the delicate trees as they sway in the warm breeze. Swans take flight in the distance as baby deer play in a field of primroses.

### SPOOKY

Lightning flashes outside the window of the deserted mansion. Cobwebs are lit for a moment and bats flutter past the window. The stair creaks and the door squeaks open. The old butler carries a candle into the room. His pale face is expressionless as the sounds of chains scraping in the hallway and distant laughter fill our ears. 'Master is ready for you now,' he says.

### LOVE

The boat moved into the sunlight, which lit up her face with a radiant beauty. He looked at her in a new way. It went beyond words, and as she raised her eyes to meet his, she knew her life would never be the same again.

### ANGER

The president slammed his fist on to the table. He had given them every chance, and still they defied his wishes. He pushed his chair back and suddenly stood to his full height. His face flushed with anger, he pointed at his secretary, his hand quivering. 'This means war,' he said.

## Activity 1    Creating mood or feeling

1    Choose one of the feelings from the six given on page 18. Read the scene description. Now look at the 'Decisions' box, which will help you to plan your composition.

2    Compose a piece of music lasting about one minute to represent fully the feelings and events in the title and scene. (You may even write your own short scene for the title if you wish.) If you are stuck for ideas, look in the glossary of 'atmospheres' on page 59.

### DECISIONS

**Instruments/voices.** Which instruments will you use? Will you need to use voice?

**Dynamics.** How loud should the piece begin? How should the dynamics develop? Should there be sudden changes?

**Tempo.** How fast should the piece begin? Should the tempo remain the same? Should it change gradually or suddenly?

**Pitch.** Should instruments play high or low?

**Texture.** How many instruments do you need at the beginning? When do other instruments join in? When do they stop? Do you need silence?

**Melody.** Do you need to compose a melody? What sort of melody should it be?

**Harmony.** Will you use chords? Do you need discords and clashes?

**Rhythm.** Does your piece need steady or sudden rhythms? Should rhythms be a main feature?

### ! TIPS

- Decide on a sound, rhythm, harmony or melody that will open your piece and set the atmosphere.
- Decide how this first idea should change or what can be added to it.
- What will be the main events in your piece? Will they be related to events in the scene?
- Decide how your piece will end. Will it return to your first idea in any way?
- Make sure that you plan your piece as carefully as possible.

## Activity 2    Performing and evaluating

Perform your piece to the class, but don't tell them which scene you chose. Class members will guess and write down the titles of the pieces they hear, with reasons for their choice. Write your piece as a graphic score along the lines of the example in Project 10 (page 24).

### Research work

1    Find out who wrote *The Planets*. What guides the composer's choice of moods and atmospheres in this piece?

2    Find out what 'programme music' is. Try to find some examples and bring them to class.

# Messages and music

## A BUGLE CALL

 *18–21*

A bugle call uses just the three notes of a triad or chord to send important messages and put across complex emotions. You are going to listen to four bugle calls. Each call is used in one of the following situations. Which call do you think matches which situation? Why?

**a)** Wake up-early morning (Reveille)

**b)** To bed, night time (Mess call)

**c)** Arrival of important visitor

**d)** Into battle

**e)** Victory

**f)** Defeat-retreat

**g)** Burial of the dead (Last post)

*Activity* **1** **Composing bugle calls**

1   Using the notes C, E and G in any order compose two short bugle calls. Your calls should be suitable for any of the situations listed above. Choose two contrasting situations.

2   Write down your bugle call. You can use either of the following.

**a)** Letters – for example:

**b)** Music notation – for example:

C   C   G C   E   G   E   C   E   G   C   G

> **! TIPS**
>
> - Keep the range of notes within an octave and a half.
> - Remember your key note (tonic) is C.
> - Adapt the following to suit the mood of your bugle call.
>   *Tempo*
>   *Upward or downward pitch movement*
>   *Length of notes*
>   *Dynamics*

3   Share your call with others.

**a)** What do they think it represents?

**b)** Now try to teach them your call.

Mobile phones use a variety of tones and melodies to send messages to the owner.

1   Using only the notes D, E, G, A and B, or a scale of your choice, invent the following.

    **a)**   A short phrase meaning 'text message received'.

    **b)**   A short phrase meaning 'battery low'.

    **c)**   A short phrase meaning 'called, number engaged'.

    **d)**   A short phrase meaning 'called, number ringing'.

    **e)**   A short phrase meaning 'alarm tone'.

2   Write down your phrases using letters (refer back to Project 2, pages 8–9 for examples) or music notation. You may wish to sequence your phrases and save them as MIDI files.

3   Using a scale of your choice or invention, compose a longer melody as your personal ring-tone.

    **a)**   Try to make your melody reflect your personality or image.

    **b)**   Select a suitable sound source for your ring-tone.

    **c)**   You may wish to sequence your result and save it as a MIDI file.

    **d)**   See if you can save your melody to your phone, or send it to someone else via e-mail.

## *Research work*

1   Find the answers to the following questions on bugle calls.

    **a)**   Are bugle calls still used in the army?

    **b)**   Where and how do military musicians train?

    **c)**   What other brass instruments are used in a military band?

2   Now answer these questions on mobile phones.

    **a)**   See if you can find melodies by classical composers in your (or a friend's) mobile phone. What are they?

    **b)**   How can ring-tone melodies can be changed and stored in mobile phones?

    **c)**   How often do you change your ring-tone?

    **d)**   Which is your favourite ring-tone and why?

# *The soldier's tale*

## THE SOLDIER'S MARCH

 23

**Text:** CIF Ramuz **English version:** Michael Flanders and Kitty Black **Music:** Igor Stravinsky

Down a hot and dusty road

Tramps a soldier with his load

Ten days leave he has to spend

Will his journey never end?

Marching home, marching on his way

Marching, marching all the day,

Soon he will be home to stay.

He's been marching all the day,

Happy now he's here to stay.

### *Activity* **1**  Reading the text

1   Read, listen to or speak the poem above.

2   What is it about? What are the feelings of the soldier?

### *Activity* **2**  Imitate and improvise

 7  3

1   Imitate and improvise over the backing on the MIDI file using the scale: **C D E F G A B C**

2   Try to give your improvisation the feel of a soldier's march.

### *Activity* **3**  Composing a march

 7  3

1   Now compose a march melody over the backing, using the same notes. Your piece should be 'a soldier's march', but you can make this march:

  a)   *cheerful* (glad to be home), or

  b)   *tired* (after his long journey).

2   Write your march down on paper.

  a)   Using letters

       If notes happen quickly put them close together. Use an arrow to indicate if you go up or down to a note.

       C CD E F G ↑ C G G GF E D C ↓ G C

> **! TIPS**
>
> • Make your melody a fixed length – perhaps four or eight bars, or four beats per bar.
>
> • Consider how the following can make your march sound 'cheerful' or 'tired'.
>
>   *Long or short notes.*
>
>   *A fast- or slow-moving tune.*
>
>   *A wide or narrow range of notes.*
>
>   *Upward or downward pitch movement.*
>
>   *By using B♭ or E♭ in your scale.*

**b)** Using notation

3 Now play your melody to the class or share it with a friend.

---

**Activity 4    Composing a melody for words**

 7 3

1 Listen to, play or sing the melody below, which sets part of the poem to music. This melody has been composed over a backing (MIDI file 4) and uses the scale: **C D E F G A B♭ C**.

**a)** Using letters

```
C  D  E  F  G  G  A
```
Down a hot and du-sty road

```
 B♭ B♭ A  G  F  A  G
```
Tramps a sol-dier with his load

```
 G  G  F  E  D  C  D
```
Ten days leave he has to spend

```
 C  D  E  D C B♭ C
```
Will his jour-ney e-ver end?

**b)** Using notation

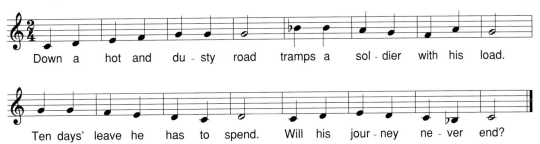

Down a    hot and    du – sty    road    tramps a    sol – dier    with    his    load.

Ten days' leave he    has    to    spend.    Will    his    jour – ney    ne – ver    end?

2 Invent your own melody for the words, using the scale of: **C D E (E♭) F G A B (B♭) C**.

Write it down on paper using either letters or notation. You may be asked to perform your piece to other class members.

---

 **Research work**

1 Find out about Igor Stravinsky. When and where did he live? What were his most famous compositions?

2 Find out the whole story of *The soldier's tale*.

3 Research why music been important for armies. When and for what purposes do armies use music?

4 Try to find the names – composers or music – of any famous marches.

# Graphic soundscapes

## GRAPHIC SCORES

| | 1 | 2 | 3 | 4 | 5 | 6 | 7 | 8 | 9 | 10 | 11 | 12 |
|---|---|---|---|---|---|---|---|---|---|---|---|---|
| Door | | ↻ open | | ↺ close | | | ↻ open | | ↺ close | ↻ open | E | |
| Cough/ Sneeze | | | | ᴜᴜᴜ | | | | ᴜᴜᴜᴜ | ☀ sneeze | ☀ sneeze | C | |
| Twanging Ruler | | | 〰 < > | | | | 〰 < > | | 〰 < > | 〰 < > | N | |
| Teacher Voice | SWB? (mp) | | | | SWB? (mf) | | | | | SWB? (f) | E | SWB? (mp) |
| Pupil Voice 1 | | | SIL (f) | | | | | SIL (f) | | SIL (f) | E | |
| Pupil Voice 2 | | | | | | ! (mf) | | | ! (f) | ! (f) | L | |
| Piano | CHORD 1 ♩ (mp) ⟋ | | | | CHORD 2 ♩ (mf) ⟋ | | | CHORD 3 ♩ ♩ (mf) | ♩ ♩ | ♩ > | I | |
| Low Drum | ♩ (mp) | | | | ♩ ♩ (mf) | | | ♩ ♩ (mf) | ♩ ♩ | ♩ > | S | |

The classroom

**Key to the graphic score**

| | | | |
|---|---|---|---|
| ↻ | Open door | SWB? | 'Shall we begin?' |
| ↺ | Close door | SIL | 'Sorry I'm late.' |
| ᴜ | Cough | ! | 'Sir, he's got my ruler!' |
| ☀ | Sneeze | Chord 1 | **Chord** of C (C E G) |
| 〰 | Twanging ruler | Chord 2 | Chord of Cm (C E♭ G) |
| Small print (p) | Quietly | Chord 3 | **Discord** (F F# B) |
| Large print (f) | Loud | ⟋ | **Diminuendo** |
| ⟍ | **Crescendo** | > | Accent the note |
| | | ♩ | Play once |

## Activity 1   Performing the graphic score

1. Look at the graphic score on page 24. The numbers across the top of the columns on the grid represent time passing. Each number represents about $1\frac{1}{2}$ seconds in this composition. The sounds used are listed in the left-hand column. The key explains what the sounds are and how they are performed. To perform the piece you should do the following.

   a) Allocate one person per sound.

   b) Each performer should practise his/her sound and notice at which numbers it occurs.

   c) One person should conduct, marking the beats with a clear gesture.

   d) The conductor may need to count out loud in rehearsal, but should be silent in the performance.

## Activity 2   Composing a graphic score

You will need a large sheet of paper on which to write your graphic score. Use the example on page 24 to help you model your own.

1. Select one of the following titles:
   - 'The classroom'
   - 'Early morning'
   - 'In the city'
   - 'The storm'
   - 'Into space'
   - 'The countryside'
   - 'Waterfall'
   - 'The haunted house'
   - 'The factory'
   - 'Family holiday'

2. In the first vertical column of your score, list the sounds sources you have chosen. You can select these from:
   - classroom instruments
   - voices
   - real sounds available in the classroom.

3. Compose your graphic score to represent your title. Your composition should last for at least twelve counts. You should decide how fast your piece will be counted before you begin to compose.

4. Provide a key to explain how you want your sounds to be played. (Use the example on page 24 to help you model your own.) Use colour to make the parts and sounds stand out.

5. You may be asked to perform your score to other class members.

> **TIPS**
> - Add musical elements (like the piano and drum in 'The classroom') that will add feeling and atmosphere to the piece.
> - Don't feel you have to fill up every space on your score! Vary the texture – and use silence.
> - When other people perform your piece you will need to conduct.

# Winter weather

## A WEEK OF WINTER WEATHER

On Monday icy rains poured down
and flooded drains all over town.

Tuesday's gales rent elm and ash;
dead branches came down with a crash.

On Wednesday, bursts of hail and sleet;
no one walked along our street.

Thursday stood out clear and calm
but the sun was paler than my arm.

Friday's frost that bit your ears
was cold enough to freeze your tears.

Saturday's sky was ghostly grey;
We smashed ice on the lake today.

Christmas Eve was Sunday and
snow fell like foam across the land.

*by* **Wes Magee**

---

**Activity 1**   **Listening to audio examples**  *24–8*

You are going to listen to some audio files. Some are pieces of music and some are sound effects. When you have heard them, answer the following questions.

1   Which files are sound effects and which are music?

2   What do the extracts represent?

3   How do you know which extracts are music?

4   What extra qualities does music add in describing the effect of weather?

5   Does music sometimes include imitation of the sound of weather?

---

**Activity 2**   **Setting the poem to music**

Use the composing tips on page 27 to set part of 'A week of winter weather' to music.

1   Make your music long enough to set the scene properly and fully describe the weather. Each verse should last at least one minute. Make music rather than sound effects, although you may want to represent real sounds sometimes.

2   Write down or record your ideas as they develop. Clearly decide when and where the poem should be read in relation to the music. Plan the piece and decide which instruments you require. Now begin the composing process.

3   Perform your piece to the rest of the class.

# COMPOSING TIPS

**Monday**

Notice that the rain is icy and pouring down. Your piece could start with constant, icy rainfall, which becomes heavier then develops into a flood. Think about:

- whether you will need to introduce new instruments as the flood begins
- whether the pitch and dynamics will remain the same
- whether the pentatonic scale might be useful to represent rainfall
- which tuned percussion would be helpful in suggesting icy rain.

**Tuesday**

Gales rise and fall in strength, with strong gusts and quieter moments. Crescendos and diminuendos using cymbal rolls and drum rolls (soft beaters) could be useful. Rapid chromatic scales are sometimes used to represent wind. 'Rent' means split. Think about:

- how you will put over this sense of sudden splitting in the midst of the gales
- how many crashes of the branches there will be
- how you will surprise the listeners.

**Wednesday**

Think about the difference between hail, sleet and rain, and how you can put across the strength and iciness of hail. Shakers, maracas and metallic sounds might help. The hail and sleet come in bursts, so silence may be an important part of this section. Remember that the hail and sleet will fall for more than a few seconds and with varying intensity. The second line provides a contrast – think about whether you could set this to music.

**Thursday**

There is a break in the weather. Think about how you can best convey this sense of calm. Slow tempi, more gentle sounds and perhaps soft sustained chords will help. Don't forget, it's still winter – so try to add a sense of eerie calm and anticipation of the return of bad weather.

**Friday**

Create a frosty scene of some length. The frost 'bites', so include jagged, brittle icy sounds that try to convey this and how it can be a danger. Metallic sounds, staccato notes and brief discords may help. Frost also shimmers in the sunlight, so you might want to create a more gentle and constant background shimmering sound against which the frost 'bites'.

**Saturday**

The sky is now grey but also ghostly. Think of a dull winter's day with an overcast sky. Slow, low repeating rhythms and soft minor chords might work. Think about how you will add the ghostly feeling to this. As the music progresses, think about:

- how you will add the effect of suddenly breaking ice
- what instrument you will choose
- how often you should repeat this effect.

**Sunday**

Snow appears for the first time. The theme or scale could be related to the rain, but it falls 'like foam', gently and weightlessly, so it won't need the power of the rain or the iciness of the hail. Think about the instruments that could best convey this. Remember the snow is 'falling', so some descent in pitch might work. Think about how you can subtly convey a sense of it being Christmas. Sleigh bells and fragments of a carol are perhaps all that's required.

# Music and media (1)

## THE QUIZ SHOW

**ANSWER THE QUESTION OR PAY THE PRICE!**

*The TV quiz where there's **big money** to win but a **price to pay** if you get the wrong answer!*

The show is hosted by retired soap star Ted Cheddar and former model Gloria Void.
You will need to study the producer's music brief below before you do Activity 1.

### The producer's music brief

1 **Theme tune**

Duration 40 seconds

Must grab audience's attention but also have a feeling of urgency!
So the sense of a clock ticking and possible danger building are
important. Almost as if a time bomb could go
off! In general, a build-up of tension and excitement.

2 **Entry of Gloria and Ted**

Duration 6 seconds

Here come the stars! Aren't they marvellous!

3 **The contestant takes the stand**

Duration 6 seconds

Suspense-tension-doom-footsteps. Going to the gallows?

4 **The question is being asked and we are waiting for the answer**

Duration For the question,
about 5 seconds; for the
answer, up to 20 seconds
depending on the time it
takes to answer

For the question, the music must be quiet but dangerous,
so we can hear the question but know that something
dangerous is happening. As we wait for the answer we must
feel the tension mount and time passing until we find out
whether the answer is right or wrong.

5 **Correct answer**

Duration 3 seconds

Hooray! Relief! Congratulations!

6 **Incorrect answer**

Duration 3 seconds

Whoops! That wasn't too clever!

7 **Penalty for three wrong answers**

Duration 5 seconds

A barrel of goo and gunk is emptied over the contestant.
So the music must show rapid falling, a sense of sliminess
and a sense of something very silly happening.

8 **Cash reward for three correct answers**

Duration 5 seconds

Delight and joy as 1000 bank notes flutter down
on to the delighted contestant.

## Activity 1   Composing music for a quiz show

You have been commissioned to write the music for a TV quiz show. The programme will require more than just theme music. Using the producer's brief on the opposite page, compose music for the various parts of the show. In each case you should think about the following.

- **Instruments.** Which would be best for the mood or atmosphere you are trying to create?
- **Dynamics.** How loud should the music be? How should the dynamics develop?
- **Tempo.** Should the music be fast or slow, or should the tempo change?
- **Rhythm.** Should the rhythms be strong, gentle, energetic, frightening, pounding, steady?
- **Melody.** What kind of melodies should you create to achieve the right atmosphere? Does every section need a melody?
- **Harmony and discord.** When should the chords and harmonies be pleasing and cheerful? When do you need discords?

## Activity 2   Performing your compositions

1   Either record your compositions or perform them to the class.

2   You may wish to perform the pieces while other members of the class act out the show. If you have recorded your pieces, they could be used in a drama lesson.

3   Evaluate you own and others' compositions. If you were the show's producer, would the compositions meet the requirements of your commission?

### Research work

1   Watch a real TV quiz show. Describe in detail how music is used to enhance the programme.

2   Choose two television advertisements. How do they use music? Is the music specially composed for the advert? What does it add to the power and meaning of the advertisement?

# Words and Music

## USING WORDS

1  Earth that gives for all to share,
   Sun-light, wa-ter food and air
   Land and ri-vers, winds and tides,
   Na-ture gives and no-thing hides.

2  Man has come to plough the land,
   Oak and ash fall at his hand,
   Land and o-cean give their store,
   Man-kind takes and asks for more.

3  Li-ving on this com-mon ground,
   We must care for what we've found.
   Catch the rain-bow in your soul,
   Hope and love will con-quer all.

---

**Activity 1**   Setting words to a rhythm and melody    8–10

1  Speak the words of the poem above over any of the suggested MIDI backings so that they fit.
   You may find it useful to write out the poem and mark the strong (accented) syllables like
   this:

   /  ◡  /  ◡  /  ◡  /
   Earth that gives for all to share

2  When you are happy that the words fit, compose a melody over the backing, using the rhythm
   you have developed, either by singing or by using the scale C–C (white notes only).

3  Write down or record your composition.

---

**Activity 2**   Developing pieces from single words    29–30

1  Now compose a piece based on *one* of the following words.

| Alleluia | Amen | Thunder | Confusion | Moonlight |
|---|---|---|---|---|

   **a)**  You can involve as many people as you wish.

   **b)**  You can repeat the word as often as you need.

   **c)**  You can sing, shout, chant or whisper the words.

   **d)**  You can use instruments or instruments and voices.

   **e)**  Think of the sound, meaning and rhythm of your chosen word as you compose.

**2** You should record your compositions. You may also be asked to do some more formal writing.

**3** You may find it helpful to listen to the examples on the CD. Notice how the composers spread out the word 'Alleluia' to make long pieces of music, giving each syllable of the word many notes (melisma) or repeating it rhythmically.

Audio file 29 is from a Gregorian chant.

Audio file 30 is from Handel's 'Hallelujah Chorus' from *The Messiah*.

## Activity 3  Free composition from words

**1** Use either of the examples below as the starting point for a composition. You can repeat, chop up, sing or chant the phrases as you wish. Try layering voices and chanting small sections of the words.

**a)**  Round about the cauldron go;

In the poisoned entrails throw.

Hubble, bubble, toil and trouble,

Fire burn and cauldron bubble!

*from* **Macbeth by William Shakespeare**

 **31**

**b)**

| | Translation |
|---|---|
| Con-fu-ta-tis ma-le-dic-tis | When the wicked are confounded, |
| Flam-mis ac-ri-bus a-dic-tis | Doomed to flames of endless misery |
| Vo-ca Me cum ben-e-dic-tis | Call me with thy saints surrounded |

These words are on audio file 31 in a setting from *Requiem* by Mozart. Notice that the first two lines contrast strongly with line 3.

 **Research work**

**1** Bring in to class examples of any of the following.

  **a)** A song from a musical.

  **b)** A pop song.

  **c)** An aria from an opera.

  **d)** An example of rap or MC-ing.

**2** Listen to them and compare them. Note down:

  **a)** how they are different

  **b)** how they are similar.

# *Music and media (2)*

## THEME MUSIC FOR TV SHOWS

The schedule for next season's new TV shows has just been announced, and you have been commissioned to write a theme for one of these programmes.

*FRESH BYTES*

An up-to-the-minute programme about the latest innovations in computers.

*SCRAP AND TWIDDLE*

More fun and antics from this hilarious pair of cartoon hamsters!

*NEWS AT 5 ON 6*

A new time for Channel 6's award-winning news bulletin.

*WASSUP!*

DJ Skat and Mr E Mix pass the mic for an hour of the freshest music.

*ANTIQUES WORLD*

Cyril Bainbridge visits the homes of the rich and famous to marvel at, and explain, their antiques.

*VOICES FROM THE UNKNOWN SHORE*

A three-part horror mystery, which begins as a family from the city arrive in a remote fishing village.

*NEWTON'S LAW*

The first episode of a space thriller, following Blake Newton's inter-galactic law enforcement team.

## Activity 1  Composing TV themes

You have been commissioned to write the theme music for some of next season's new programmes. Choose titles from the opposite page and compose themes lasting between 90 seconds and two minutes. You should consider the following when composing your piece.

- **Style.** What type or style of music would best suit your chosen programme?
- **Instruments.** Which instruments will best suit your theme? Percussion, electronic, keyboard, orchestral?
- **Dynamics and tempo.** The speed and volume of your piece will be important in setting the right mood.
- **Words.** Will you use words from the title in your theme? Will they be spoken or sung?
- **Melody.** A memorable tune could really help your theme music.
- **Harmony and discord.** Should your piece use major or minor chords? Should it use pleasing harmonies or discord and dissonance?
- **Rhythm.** Will rhythm be an important part of your piece? What sort of mood should it create?

## Activity 2  Performing your theme tune

1 Perform your theme tune to the class or record it. Let others guess which theme tune you have chosen.

2 How successful was your piece? Did you manage to put across the character of the programme? Which compositions by other students were successful? What made them effective?

 **Research work**

1 Choose the theme music from two television programmes. Describe the music in detail and say how appropriate it is to the programme content.

2 Using the music from real TV programmes, compare the theme music from:
   a) a comedy
   b) a news programme
   c) a children's programme
   d) a sports programme.

   How are they different? How do they get the viewer's attention? How do they set the right mood for the programme?

3 See if you can find any CDs of TV themes. Which themes are available? Why would people want to buy such recordings?

# Pictures at an exhibition

## SETTING THE SCENE

Look carefully at the sequence of three pictures below, and the individual pictures on the opposite page.

What do the pictures show? What feelings, moods or atmospheres do they suggest?

Choose one picture, or the three picture race sequence.

Compose a piece of music, lasting at least one minute, inspired by what you see.

# Telling the story

## SOURCES OF INSPIRATION

### DREAMTIME

In the beginning the earth was an endless plain in endless night. There were neither sun, moon, nor stars. In this shadowy twilight, lumps of shapeless matter waited for the possibility of life. Underneath the earth's crust the Sun, moon and stars glistened waiting for the moment they would emerge. On the first morning of the first day, the Sun broke through the crust of the Earth, spreading golden light across the land, warming the bodies of the Ancients. Gradually the Ancients felt life move through them as they slowly moved first one leg then the other. Each drowsing ancestor felt the Sun's warmth on his eyes. Snakes, parrots, ants, flowers and people took shape on the warming earth. Life had begun.

***adapted from* Aboriginal Creation Story**

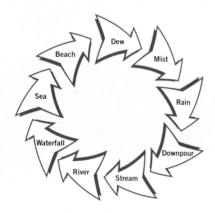

### THE SORCERER'S APPRENTICE

The sorcerer orders his lazy apprentice to fill the cauldron while he is out. Then the sorcerer leaves. The day is hot so the lazy apprentice has an idea! He casts a spell on the broom to fetch water while he rests. The broom sprouts legs and arms. It picks up buckets and starts to fill the cauldron. Then the apprentice chops the broom. With each chop more brooms are created. An army of brooms is now marching, filling the cauldron with water. The apprentice falls asleep. He suddenly wakes with water flooding everywhere. In panic, he unsuccessfully tries to stop the brooms. The sorcerer returns. He makes a powerful spell to return everything to normal. The apprentice is now in trouble!

### THE MACHINE

Slowly the machine began its repetitive grinding and clanking. As the machine accelerated, with new layers of sound and rhythm, each worker was forced to move in time. After a few moments, the machine was running at speed with the whole hall engulfed in the layers of mechanical noise. Suddenly the machine, which appeared by now to be running too fast, juddered, stalled, and ground to a halt.

## Activity 1    Composing from a story

1   Choose one of the four stories in this project and use it as a starting point for a composition.

2   Read your chosen story again, identifying the main events, characters and mood. You could draw a storyboard.

3   Decide what instruments you will use to show each event. Think about how you will create the mood.

4   Now compose a piece of music for each part of the story. For example, for 'The Sorcerer's Apprentice' you might compose a piece for each of the following musical themes.

> The Sorcerer    The Apprentice    Having an idea!    Casting a spell
> The march of the brooms    Falling asleep    Chopping wood    Flooding

## Activity 2    Choosing your own story

1   Choose a favourite book or computer game, or a story you have written.

2   Write short themes or melodies to represent at least two of the characters from the story or game.

3   Find an incident or event to set to music.

4   Write down the main events of the story, as has been done for 'The Sorcerer's Apprentice'.

5   Compose a piece of music lasting no more than 90 seconds to represent the characters and main events in the story.

6   Perform your piece to the class or record it.

### Research work

1   Discover themes and story lines for any of the following pieces of music:
   a)  *Till Eulenspiegel*
   b)  *Peter and the wolf*
   c)  *Scheherezade.*

2   Find some other examples of instrumental music that tell a story. Make a list of them.

3   Find some examples in computer games of music that helps in telling the story or that represents characters well.

# Composing with chords

## THE 'CHORD WORKOUT'

Take a look at the chords below. Your teacher will help you to play these to a variety of rhythms and patterns. This will help you with the activities in this project.

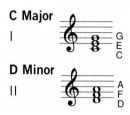

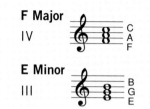

---

### Activity 1   Composing for a set chord sequence

1   Choose any of the chord sequences below and compose your own way of playing them. For example, you could:

**a)**   compose your own rhythm or pattern for the chords

**b)**   choose to use block chords or arpeggios, or a mixture

**c)**   change the order of notes in the chord

**d)**   choose a tempo and level of dynamics

**e)**   add notes to the chord.

Repeat each section as many times as you wish.

**a)**

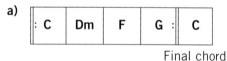

Final chord

**b)**

| :Am | G | F | G :‖ | Am |
|---|---|---|---|---|

Final chord

**c)**

Final chord

**d)**

| : C | G | Am | Em | F | C | F | G :‖ | C |
|---|---|---|---|---|---|---|---|---|

Final chord

2   Give your composition a title based on the mood you are creating.

3   Perform your piece to other class members or record it.

## Activity **2**  Chord variations

1 Compose or choose a short chord sequence (either four or eight bars). How many different ways can you play the sequence? Look at 'Choices' below for ideas.

2 Create a set of variations on your chord sequence.

   **a)** How many variations will be in your piece?

   **b)** Will some variations repeat?

   **c)** How can you make your piece have shape, balance and structure?

> **CHOICES**
>
> Tempo   Dynamics   Block chord or arpeggio?   Order of notes played
> Adding notes to the chords   One section or more?   Order of sections

3 Perform and record your piece.

## Activity **3**  Chord composition

1 Compose your own chord sequence. If you know more chords than those we have used so far in this project, feel free to use them.

2 Once you have decided on your chord sequence, think about how you will play it. You will need to give your piece a title. Remember to think about the 'Choices' to create the mood you want.

3 You may be asked to perform your piece, record it, or teach it to a friend.

### ! TIPS

- Begin and end with C if you would like your piece in a major key.
- Begin and end with Am if you would like your piece in a minor key.
- Use units of four, eight, twelve or sixteen bars.
- Your composition can have more than one section – for example, A B A or verse-chorus.
- Cadences can work well at the end of sections.
  *A perfect cadence is V–I (G–C).*
  *A plagal cadence is IV–I (F–C).*

### ? Research work

 32–3

1 Find the chord sequence of any current pop song. You may need to search the Internet, as well as look in books.

2 Find out what the chords I, II, III, IV, V, VI would be in G major, D major and F major. See if you can play and compose in any of these keys.

3 Try to find the titles, composers or recordings of any famous sets of 'variations'.

4 Listen to Bach *Prelude in C* and Beethoven *Moonlight Sonata* (audio files 32 and 33). How do composers use chords in these compositions? Do they use more than just chords?

# Melody over chords (1)

## CHORD FRAMEWORKS

Below are some chord frameworks. These frameworks will be used in the activities in this project.

**A**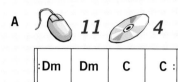

| :Dm | Dm | C | C : |
|-----|-----|---|-----|

**B**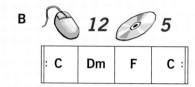

| : C | Dm | F | C : |
|-----|-----|---|-----|

**C**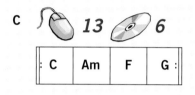

| : C | Am | F | G : |
|-----|-----|---|-----|

**D**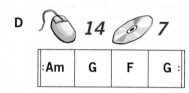

| :Am | G | F | G : |
|-----|---|---|-----|

**A1**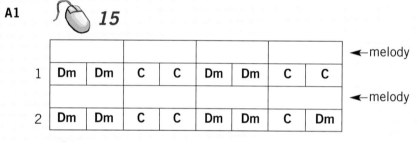

|   |    |    |   |   |    |    |   |   | ←melody |
|---|----|----|---|---|----|----|---|---|---------|
| 1 | Dm | Dm | C | C | Dm | Dm | C | C | |
|   |    |    |   |   |    |    |   |   | ←melody |
| 2 | Dm | Dm | C | C | Dm | Dm | C | Dm | |

**B1**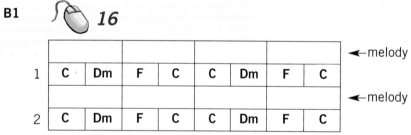

|   |   |    |   |   |   |    |   |   | ←melody |
|---|---|----|---|---|---|----|---|---|---------|
| 1 | C | Dm | F | C | C | Dm | F | C | |
|   |   |    |   |   |   |    |   |   | ←melody |
| 2 | C | Dm | F | C | C | Dm | F | C | |

**C1**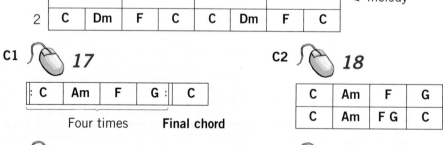

| : C | Am | F | G : | C |
|-----|-----|---|-----|---|

Four times     **Final chord**

**C2**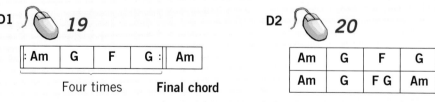

| C | Am | F | G |
|---|-----|-----|---|
| C | Am | F G | C |

**D1**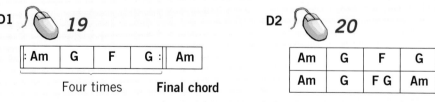

| :Am | G | F | G : | Am |
|-----|---|---|-----|----|

Four times     **Final chord**

**D2**

| Am | G | F | G |
|----|---|-----|----|
| Am | G | F G | Am |

## Activity 1    Developing a 'sequence' over chords

1   Look at chord framework **A** on page 40. Play slow scales within this repeating chord framework, as directed by your teacher.

2   Now compose a melody over the two D minor bars in framework **A**. When the melody is fixed, repeat it one note lower over the two C major bars.

3   Practise changing between the two versions of the melody as the chords change.

4   Perform your melodies to other class members or record them.

5   Now use your melodies to fit over chord framework **A1**.

6   Perform and record your melody. If you can, write it down on a grid similar to the ones used on page 40.

## Activity 2    Composing more sequences and melodies

1   Take a look at chord framework **B**. Now follow steps 1 to 4 in Activity 1, but in this case you will take your phrase up one from C to Dm, then up two to F, then back to where you started.

2   Make up your own piece that lasts for four repetitions of the sequence. Use a grid like the one in **B1** to write down your melody above the chords.

## Activity 3    Freedom within chord changes

Many melodies are not always created from 'sequences', but rely on the instincts of the composer. Improvise freely over the chord sequences in frameworks **C** and **D**, relying on the 'feel' of what is right, rather than exactly what notes make up the chord.

## Activity 4    Composing a four-line melody

Compose a four-line melody over any of the four-line chord sequences shown in frameworks **C1**, **C2**, **D1** or **D2**.

### ! TIPS

- Use only white notes.
- Develop your sequences by 'feel' from the improvisations you have done.
- Remember to repeat phrases and rhythms in your melody.
- You used the structure A A B A in Project 4 (see pages 12–13). Think about how you could structure your melody here.

# Drones (1)

## EXAMPLES OF DRONES

A drone is a note, or group of notes, held as a bass throughout a piece of music.

Thirteenth-century dance, 'The song of the ass'    21   13

Drone note: G (with D)

'Danse Royale'    22

Drone note: A (with E)

Pedal bass pop riff    23

## Activity 1   Performing 'The song of the ass' 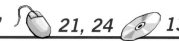 21, 24   13

1    Listen to the thirteenth-century dance tune (music on page 42) with the drone backing (MIDI file 21). Which instrumental sounds will be suitable for playing the drone and melody in a dance piece from the medieval period?

2    Now perform the drone (G and D) to a variety of rhythms.

3    Next, learn to play the melody. When you have learned it, perform the melody with the recorded drone backing (MIDI file 24). If you wish, you can perform the drone and the percussion parts live. Find interesting ways of playing the drone.

4    A second example, 'Danse Royale', also appears on page 42. This is recorded as MIDI file 22.

## Activity 2   Composing a medieval dance  24, 25

1    Over the MIDI file backing 24, compose your own piece in the style of a medieval dance.

2    Perform your piece with the MIDI backing or as a group where there are drone and percussion players as well as melody parts. Give the drone part interesting rhythms and patterns. Be sure to choose appropriate sounds.

3    The backing to 'Danse Royale' is MIDI file 25, if you would like to work with this.

### ! TIPS

- Your tonic is G, and you use only white notes.
- Make your piece lively and suitable for dance.
- The thirteenth-century dance on page 42 uses two-bar phrases that imitate each other.

## Activity 3   Composing over a pedal bass  23

Pedal bass works like a drone. A single bass note is held, while the chords change over the top.

1    Listen to the 'pedal bass' pop riff example. What is the held bass note? Can you spot when the chords change?

2    Play along with the MIDI file backing. You could play the bass note, the chords or both.

3    Use the backing to invent your own piece over the top. It could be a song or an instrumental. It could have more than one section. Your tonic is A and you can use just white notes.

###  Research work

1    Find out as much as you can about medieval dance music. Who was it composed for? Who wrote it? What instruments were used?

2    Look for songs or parts of songs that use pedal bass. Make a list of the ones you find.

# Melody over chords (2)

## NOTING YOUR IDEAS

| Melody | $\begin{smallmatrix}\text{EDCD}\end{smallmatrix}$ (staff) | | | Write in your melody here | | | |
|---|---|---|---|---|---|---|---|
| Upper harmony note | G | | One note from the chord of each bar | | | | |
| Lower harmony note | E | | Another note from the chord of each bar | | | | |
| Bar number | 1 | 2 | 3 | 4 | 5 | 6 | 7 | 8 |
| Chord | C | F | G | C | Am | F | G | C |
| Notes in chord | G̶ E̶ C | Write in the letter names of each chord. Cross them out as you use them. | | | | | | |

---

### Activity 1    Composing a melody over backing  26

You will need a large sheet of paper on which to write your melody over the backing. Use the example above to help you model your own.

1 Compose a melody over the first four bars of the MIDI file backing, which will be repeated many times.

Chords:

| C | F | G | C |
|---|---|---|---|

> **! TIPS**
> - You can use all the notes from the scale of C (all white notes).
> - Improvise with these notes until you play something that fits well.
> - Use the notes of the chord as a guide, particularly if you come to rest on a note. The tonic (key note) is C.

**2** Now continue the melody for bars 5 to 8. Your teacher will loop the backing so you can improvise.

Chords:

| Am | G | F | C |
|----|---|---|---|

**TIPS**

- Make the second half of your melody continue smoothly from the first half.
- Base it on ideas from bars 1 to 4.

**3** When your melody is complete, perform it to other class members.

## Activity 2    Arranging from chords

**1** Write down the letter names of the three notes in each chord in the box marked 'Notes in chord' on page 44. Cross them off as you use them. This will be your guide to the notes you can use in the 'harmony note' parts.

**2** Compose two held harmony note parts (upper and lower), which could be played on 'strings' or any other soft, sustained sound.

   **a)** First, choose notes for the 'upper harmony' part, using 'Rules' below.

   **b)** Next, choose notes for the 'lower harmony' part. The rules are the same, except the note should be different to the upper harmony note.

> RULES
> - Only choose a note from the chord of that bar.
> - Choose a note that is near to, or the same as, the one you chose in the previous bar.

## Activity 3    Performing a group arrangement of the piece

A group could perform the following arrangement.

- Student 1 – melody.
- Student 2 – upper harmony.
- Student 3 – lower harmony.
- Student 4 – bass line (bottom note of chord).
- Student 5 – chords.

## Research work

Choose a pop song, then see if you can answer the following questions.

**1** Which instruments or voices sustain individual notes from chords?

**2** Which instruments play whole chords?

**3** How are those chords played? Rhythmically? Arpeggios?

**4** Who has the melody?

# Twelve-bar blues

## PLAYING THE BLUES

**a)** The blues chord **sequence**

| 1<br>**C** | 2<br>**C** | 3<br>**C** | 4<br>**C** |
|---|---|---|---|
| 5<br>**F** | 6<br>**F** | 7<br>**C** | 8<br>**C** |
| 9<br>**G** | 10<br>**F** | 11<br>**C** | 12<br>**G** |

**b)** Blues scales for improvising and melody writing (tonic is C)

**Blues scale 1**

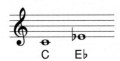

C   Eb

**Blues scale 2**

Bb  C  D  Eb  F

**Blues scale 3**

Bb  C  D  Eb  (E)  F  F♯  G

**c)** A blues bass line

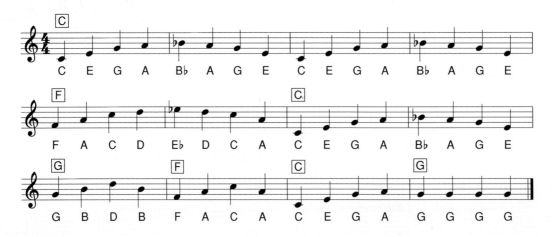

C  E  G  A  Bb  A  G  E  C  E  G  A  Bb  A  G  E

F  A  C  D  Eb  D  C  A  C  E  G  A  Bb  A  G  E

G  B  D  B  F  A  C  A  C  E  G  A  G  G  G  G

**d)** The full blues scale

C  D  Eb  (E)  F  (F♯)  G  A  Bb  (B)  C

## Activity 1    Twelve-bar blues chord sequence     27–8  8

1   Learn to play the chords C, F and G. Practise changing between these chords.

2   Practise the twelve-bar blues sequence, remembering that each bar of the sequence is worth four beats. When you are confident with the chord changes, play the chords in time with the MIDI backing.

3   Experiment with playing the chords to a variety of rhythms. Now invent your own rhythms and ways of playing the chords with the sequence.

## Activity 2    Composing over the sequence    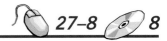 27–8 8

1   Imitate and improvise over the MIDI backing. Start with blues scale 1 on page 46. You may progress to blues scale 2 or 3.

2   Compose a short (one- or two-bar) repeating phrase, using notes from either blues scale 1 or 2. This phrase will probably fit over all twelve bars of the sequence.

3   Your two-bar phrase may not fit so well over the last line of the blues sequence. If so, try varying it slightly for these last four bars.

> **! TIPS**
>
> Your blues melody will work best like this.
> - Line 1 (four bars) – melody A.
> - Line 2 (four bars) – melody A.
> - Line 3 (four bars) – melody B.

4   Now compose your own twelve-bar blues melody, using any notes of the blues scale.

## Activity 3    A twelve-bar blues bass line    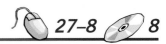 27–8 8

1   Listen to and learn the bass line on the MIDI file in small sections. Notice how it is based around the chords of the blues, using arpeggios.

2   When you can play the bass line, practise performing it against the blues chords.

3   Now compose your own bass line for the twelve-bar sequence. This can be based around notes from each chord – especially the root note.

## Research work

1   Research where and when the blues originated.

2   Find out as much as you can about some important blues performers.

3   Research the answers to the following questions.
   a)   What is a 'blue' note?
   b)   Why is the blues originally associated with personal sadness?
   c)   Which instruments are particularly associated with the blues?
   d)   What connection are there (if any) between the blues and pop music?

## PROJECT (22)

# Drones (2)

## INDIAN RAGS

Indian Rags (pronounced raag – with a long 'a') are scales from India. They are associated with particular times and moods. Thats are simplified versions of Rags. Traditional and classical Indian music is usually played over a drone.

a) Rag Bhupali (night time – peace)

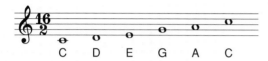

**Bhupali**

Tonic/drone note C

(Second drone note G)

**Small group of notes for composing:**

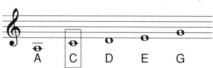

b) That Bhairav (morning)

**Bhairav**

Tonic/drone note E

(Second drone note B)

**Small group of notes for composing:**

c) Rag Yaman (early evening Rag)

**Yaman**

Tonic/drone note D

(Second drone note A)

**Small group of notes for composing:**

## Activity 1    Exploring Indian Rags

1   Choose one of the Rags on page 48. Using a suitable sound – for example flute, sitar or harmonium – play through the scale you have chosen.

    **a)**   Explore the notes and intervals of the scale.

    **b)**   Improvise without a beat, freely.

2   Using a small group of notes from the scale, improvise until you compose a short melody of about four to eight notes. This is your *gat* (whch means 'short composed melody').

## Activity 2    Improvising over the drone

 *29–31*

Use the MIDI backing for your chosen scale and play your melody in time with it. Then begin to improvise around it.

## Activity 3    Structuring your composition

1   Choose one of these two structures for your composition.

    **a)**   *Alaap* – free improvisation, without backing, where you explore the notes and character of the scale and its mood. You can linger on notes and perform as freely as you like.

    **b)**   *Jor* – the backing begins. Play your *gat* as many times as you wish. Improvise around your melody. Improvise freely in the scale. This is the *Jhalla* (climax) of the piece.

### ! TIPS

- Play fragments of your melody, repeating them.
- Play your melody at half speed.
- Play your melody at double speed.
- Decorate the notes with short trills and extra notes.
- Improvise freely in your chosen scale, returning to your melody from time to time.

2   Perform your composition using a live backing.

    **a)**   If you do not have tabla, use bongos and a hand drum.

    **b)**   For your drone use the tonic/drone note as your main note, with the second drone note played more quietly or less often.

    **c)**   The drone can be played using sitar, harmonium or string bass, or a combination of these.

### ? Research work

1   Find out the main instruments used in Indian music.

2   Research what 'Bollywood' is and why music is important for it.

3   Find examples of modern pop that use the sounds and scales of traditional Indian music.

# *Pop song*

## COMPOSING POP SONGS

This project gives you starting points and ideas to develop your own pop pieces.

---

**Activity 1**   Rhythms and bass riffs    *39–42*

1   Repeat or add to any of the following rhythms and bass riffs. They can be used as a starting point for singing, rap MCing or further instrumental work.

   **a)**   Hip-hop riff (MIDI file 39)

   **b)**   Garage riff (MIDI file 40)

   **c)**   Drum 'n' bass riff (MIDI file 41)

   **d)**   Rock riff (1) (MIDI file 42)

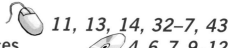

**Activity 2**   Playing with chord sequences

1   Repeat or add to the following chord sequences. They can be the basis for singing or instrumental work.

2   Add further sections and work out your own version to play as a group. If singing, try to develop your own lyrics.

   **a)   Reggae/ska** (MIDI file 11, audio file 4)
   Tonic: **D**
   Scale: **D, E, F, G, A, B♭, or B, C**

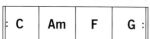

   **b)   Slow ballad (1)** (MIDI file 14, audio file 7)
   Tonic: **A**
   Scale: **A, B, C, D, E, F, G, A**

| :Am | G | F | G : |
|-----|---|---|-----|

   **c)   Slow ballad (2)** (MIDI file 13, audio file 6)
   Tonic: **C**
   Scale: **C, D, E, F, G, A, B, C**

| : C | Am | F | G : |
|-----|----|---|-----|

   **d)   Pop song** (MIDI file 32, audio file 9)
   Tonic: **C**
   Scale: **C, D, E, F, G, A, B, C**

| : Am | F | G | C : |
|------|---|---|-----|

   **e)   Pop riff (1)** (MIDI file 33, audio file 10)
   Tonic: **D**
   Scale: **D, E, F#, G, A, B (C# or C optional)**

   **f)   Soul stomp** (MIDI file 34, audio file 11)
   Tonic: **C**
   Scale: **C, D, E, F, G, A, B, C**

four times

**g) Pedal bass ballad** (MIDI file 35)
Tonic: **D**
Scale: **D, E, F#, G, A, B, C, D**

| D | C | G | D |
|---|---|---|---|
| D | | | → |

**h) Pop riff (2)** (MIDI file 36, audio file 12)
Tonic: **G**
Scale: **G, A, B, C, D, E, F, G**

| G | F | C | G |
|---|---|---|---|

**i) Descending bass pop song** (MIDI file 37)
Tonic: **C**
Scale: **C, D, E, F, G, A, B, C**

| C | G | Am | C |
|---|---|----|---|
|   | B |    | G |
| F | C | Dm | G |
|   | E |    |   |

**j) Rock riff (2)** (MIDI file 43)
Tonic: **C**
Scale: **C, D, E, F, G, A, B, C**

| D D G G | A A G G |
|---------|---------|

## *Activity* 3   A structure

Create a pop song that uses the following structure.

| | |
|---|---|
| **INTRO** | Short section using chords from the verse or chorus. |
| **VERSE 1** | First main section; the words change for each verse, but the tune stays the same. |
| **CHORUS** | Make it simple and catchy with a 'hook'; this section repeats. |
| **VERSE 2** | Same as verse 1, but with new words. |
| **CHORUS** | As before. |
| **MIDDLE** | A short contrasting section. |
| **CHORUS** | As before. |
| **CODA/OUTRO** | A short section, like the intro, to close the song. |

## Research work

1 Choose a pop song. Write down the structure using the words 'verse', 'chorus', 'middle', 'intro', 'coda' and 'bridge'. (The bridge is a short link between the main sections.)

2 Bring your favourite pop song to class. Tell the class as much as you can about the performers, why you like the song, and what instruments and voices it uses.

3 Find out as much as you can about the following pop styles:
   **a)** rock 'n' roll   **d)** Brit pop   **g)** hip hop   **j)** nu metal
   **b)** punk   **e)** Tamla Motown   **h)** rap   **k)** R 'n' B.
   **c)** glam rock   **f)** UK garage   **i)** country   **l)** soul

4 Found out how the sound is produced on a CD and how it is produced on vinyl. Why is vinyl popular with DJs?

5 Explain the following terms: **a)** hook   **b)** riff   **c)** back beat.

# Five-finger studies

## LOOKING AT STUDIES

A 'study' is a composition that helps performers to improve their playing technique. Take a look at the two pieces below. These famous tunes have been used as a study to help a keyboard player in three ways:

- to improve 'five-finger' right-hand technique
- to help someone play with both hands together
- to help a beginner with left-hand/chord playing.

**a)** Largo

Dvorak *New World Symphony*

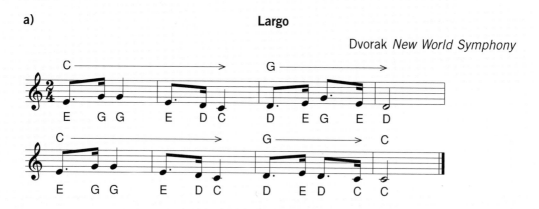

**b)** Ode to Joy

Beethoven Ninth Symphony

## Activity 1    Learning two pieces

1  Place your right hand on the keyboard in the 'five finger' position. Your thumb (finger 1) should be on C, and your little finger (finger 5) should be on G. First, learn to play either or both of the tunes on page 52 with your right hand.

2  Next, with your left hand you can add either single notes or the chords as you play your tune with the right. The left-hand notes are written above the tune.

## Activity 2    Composing a five-finger study

1  Compose your own five-finger study for keyboard. Make it no longer than the examples on page 52, and make it easy enough for others to learn. If you wish, you can base it on these examples by altering the order or rhythm of the notes.

2  See if you can work out a left-hand part for your piece – either chords or single notes.

3  Write down your piece so that others can play it.

## Activity 3    Creating studies for instrument or voice

1  Compose a study that helps to develop a technique on any instrument or the voice. Make it simple enough for you and others to play it. Give your piece a title. Here are some examples.

     a) A study for a percussion instrument that concentrates on dynamics or beater control.

     b) A study for a percussion instrument that helps to improve control of tempo changes.

     c) A study that develops chord playing on instruments.

     d) A study based on scales.

     e) A study that helps people improve co-ordination – for drum kit or piano, for example.

     f) Wind and brass players might like to create studies to improve fingering, tonguing or breath control.

     g) String players might like to compose studies to develop bowing techniques and changes of position.

     h) Students who use decks for mixing might develop a study to help others learn particular mixing or cross-fading techniques.

     i) Guitar players who use effects could develop a study for the control of effects units.

## Research work

1  Find out what an 'etude' is. Then find some examples written by famous composers.

2  Find out about Karl Czerny and his connection with studies.

3  Find out who Dvorak was and what the *New World Symphony* is.

4  Find out as much as you can about Beethoven's Ninth Symphony and *Ode to Joy*.

# *Music for film*

## THE LETTER

This project is based on three short films, which are on the CD-ROM.

### Activity 1    *The Letter:* using music to set the mood

| Time in seconds | Action |
|---|---|
| 00–10 | A woman enters a house, sees a letter on the mat and picks it up. |
| 10–36 | She moves into the room, sits down and opens the letter. |
| 36–46 | On reading the letter, she stands up and throws it on the table. |
| 46–53 | She hastily leaves the room and the house. |

1   The action in *The Letter* can be understood in two ways. Compose music for one of the versions listed below.

**1: The letter contains good news.**

The woman is hoping for, and receives, good news. She drops the letter in excitement and leaves the room overjoyed.

**2: The letter contains bad news.**

The woman is dreading bad or terrifying news. She drops the letter in distress and leaves the room upset.

2   Now choose either version 1 or version 2 and compose an appropriate piece of music to set the mood.

### Activity 2    *The Comedy Chefs:* composing music to match actions

You are going to compose a piece of music to match a sequence of actions for *The Comedy Chefs* (see video clip and below) – just like it does in a cartoon like *Tom and Jerry*. You may wish to write a comedy tune to represent the two chefs. This could be running for most of the extract and be interrupted by the music for the action.

| Time in seconds | Action |
|---|---|
| 00–30 | The chefs greet the viewers and start to work. |
| 30–2 | Chef 2 opens the cupboard door; Chef 1 bangs his head on it. |
| 32–4 | Chef 2 opens the cupboard door and hits Chef 1 in the face. |
| 35–42 | Chef 2 opens the egg box. |
| 42–9 | Chef 2 throws two eggs to Chef 1, who catches them. |
| 49–53 | Chef 1 starts to work. A third egg is thrown, which hits him. |
| 53–1.08 | Chef 2 reaches up for the flour, which eventually falls and hits Chef 1. |
| 1.08–1.22 | Chef 2 prepares and tosses the pancake upwards. |
| 1.20–1.27 | We wait for the pancake to fall. It suddenly falls onto Chef 1. |
| 1.28–1.36 | Chef 1 cleans his face. He looks upset, but then he smiles! |

**Activity** 3 ## *The Chase:* creating tension, suspense and movement

Look at *The Chase* and compose a suitable piece of music for it.

| Time in seconds | Action |
|---|---|
| 00–13 | Shots of the woods. A person walks alone, frightened. |
| 13–19 | The person is viewed from behind a bush. The camera closes in on her. |
| 19–28 | She starts to run through the woods. |
| 28–43 | She stops and looks around in panic. The woods appear to spin. |
| 44–50 | She starts to run again, in panic. |
| 50–1.06 | She stumbles and falls. She investigates what she has fallen over. |
| 1.12 | To her horror she finds she has stumbled over her own body. |
| 1.08–1.23 | Feelings of terror, as she surveys the forest scene – and her situation. |

 ## Research work

1  Find out how and why music was important in the days of silent films.

2  Find out about Bernard Herman, Hans Zimmer and Craig Armstrong.

   **a)**  For which films have they written music?

   **b)**  Find some examples of their music and make a list.

3  Find an extract from a film where you think the music is effective. Write about it, or bring the extract to class.

# References

## Common musical instruments

### Percussion

Agogo
Bongos
Cabasa
Castanets
Chime bar
Claves (sticks)
Conga
Cow bell
Cymbal
Finger cymbals
Glockenspiel
Maracas
Rain stick
Shaker
Tabla
Tam tam
Tambourine
Tone bar
Triangle
Timpani (kettle drums)
Wood block
Xylophone

### Drum kit

Bass drum
Snare drum
Hi-hat (open and closed)
Floor tom
Mid tom
Hi tom

### Pop and electronic

Guitar (electric and acoustic)
Synthesiser
Keyboard
Drum machine
Decks/turntables/mixer
Bass guitar

### Keyboard

Piano
Organ
Harpsichord
Synthesiser
Electric piano

### Brass

Trumpet
Trombone
French horn
Tuba
Euphonium

### Strings

Violin
Viola
Cello
Double bass

### Woodwind

Piccolo
Flute
Oboe
Clarinet
Bassoon
Bass clarinet

### Voices

Soprano
Alto
Tenor
Bass

# Glossary

## Glossary of musical language

**Ascend** to rise or get higher in pitch

**Canon** exact imitation of another voice or instrumental part

**Chord** two or more notes played at the same time

**Crescendo** to get gradually louder

**Descend** to fall or get lower in pitch

**Diminuendo** to get gradually quieter

**Discord** two or more notes that clash with each other when played at the same time, e.g. C and C#

**Dissonance** the effect of notes which clash in a discord

**Dynamics** the amount or intensity of volume; how loud or quiet music is

**Glissando** upward or downward slide

**Improvisation** when players improvise, they invent the music as they go along

**Legato** playing smoothly, with no gaps between the notes. The opposite of staccato

**Melody** a sequence of notes organized to make musical sense, a tune

**Metronome** a device for maintaining a steady pulse, for recording or rehearsal

**Ostinato** a repeated phrase or pattern

**Pitch** how high or low notes are

**Pizzicato** plucking strings

**Prepared piano** addition of objects and dampers to piano strings to create effects

**Rallentando (Rall.)** to gradually slow down

**Riff** short, repeated phrase or passage. Usually applied to pop music and jazz

**Roll** rapid repetition of notes on a drum

**Rondo form** music with the structure ABACADA etc.

**Round** a simple canon such as *London's Burning* or *Three Blind Mice*

**Sequence** a) the arrangement of notes or chords in a particular order as in a chord sequence b) when a melodic phrase is repeated at a higher or lower pitch

**Staccato** shortening a note; detaching it from notes in front and behind. The opposite of legato

**Sustain** to make a note last longer

**Syncopation** avoidance of strong or main beats when playing or performing

**Tempo** the speed of music, how fast or slow it is played

**Ternary form** music with the structure ABA

**Texture** the layers of sound in a piece of music, and how they work together

**Tonic** the key note or main note

**Tremolo** rapid repetition of notes on a stringed instrument

**Tune** a) a melody b) to bring a voice or instrument to a chosen pitch

**Unison** all performers sing or play the same note

**Vibrato** rapid variations in pitch, which make a note 'wobble'

# Glossary of music technology

**Aftertouch** the response of a keyboard note to pressure, after the first playing

**CDR** a recordable CD

**CDRW** a CD which can be recorded, erased and rewritten many times

**Chorus** an effect which adds body to sound by giving the impression of multiplying the voice or instrument

**EQ (Equalisation)** a filter which allows you to increase or reduce frequencies, for example to boost the 'treble' or 'bass'

**Feedback** an unpleasant, looped, whining sound caused when a microphone picks up sounds from an amp or speaker

**GM (General MIDI)** a standard MIDI format of 128 sounds and other control messages

**Line in/out** a socket for sending and receiving 'line level' signals such as keyboards and samplers

**Local on/off** when local is on, a keyboard plays its own sounds. When off, the sounds can be controlled by an external device such as a computer

**MIDI (Musical Instrument Digital Interface)** the standard interface by which musical instruments communicate with computers

**MIDI files** standard files containing songs and arrangements in MIDI format. They are sets of messages and do not contain any real sounds

**Mixer** a device which allows musicians to balance and adjust a number of sound inputs into a single stereo output

**Modulation wheel** a wheel on a synthesiser, which allows the addition of effects such as vibrato

**MP3** a format that compresses audio into files which are much smaller than WAV files

**Multitrack** a recorder (tape or digital) which can record two or more tracks of music

**Multitimbral** a keyboard or other instrument capable of playing two or more sounds at the same time

**Patch** a sound in an electronic musical instrument

**Pitchbend** a wheel on a synthesiser which allows you to alter the pitch of a sound

**Portamento** a smooth slide between two notes

**Quantise** a method of tidying up notes to the nearest chosen beat

**Reverb. (Reverberation)** an effect which recreates the effect of performing in real acoustic spaces, such as rooms, halls or cathedrals

**Sampler** a device which records sounds and allows them to be played by an instrument

**Sequencer** a multitrack recording device (hardware or software) which allows you to record and arrange MIDI and audio information

**Synthesiser** a musical instrument, usually a keyboard, which allows sounds to be created and changed electronically

**Velocity** the speed with which a key is struck on a keyboard, which affects the loudness of the note

**WAV** a standard audio file. It contains 'real' sounds, unlike MIDI files which only contain digital messages

**Waveform** the basic soundwaves which create the raw material of a sound

# Glossary of atmospheres

Some suggestions to help your composing

**Anger** short, sharp rhythms and chords. Rapid crescendos, pounding drum rolls

**Chase** short, energetic phrases, which gradually rise in pitch and get faster. Rapid movement using chromatic scales. Crescendo as chase progresses

**Church** Organ sound. Chords using suspended 4ths and plagal cadences

**Danger** rocking semitone movement (C C# C C#) as in *Jaws*. Repeating discords with unexpected accents. Changing time signatures unexpectedly. Pauses of unpredictable length. Imitation of pounding heart

**Death/funeral** slow, steady repeated rhythms, low drums, minor chords and scales. Alternating between slow Am and E chords

**Excitement** rapid rising arpeggios, bright lively rhythms

**Fear/evil** the 'Devil's interval' C-F# or F-B (the augmented 4th). Random use of the chromatic scale. Pounding drums, scraping, extremes of pitch, use of vocal sighs and groans. Panting, chanting of mystical phrases

**Industry** metallic and wooden ostinati with scrapes and rattles. An increase in dynamics and tempo as the ostinato progresses. Combination of electronic and real sounds

**Love** gentle chords played as blocks or as arpeggios with a slow moving melody

**Modernity/hi-tech** electronic sounds and robotic rhythms. Arpeggios using synthesiser sounds

**Mystery/dreamworld** use the whole tone scale (C D E F# G# A#) to create melodies, chords and drones, slow moving chords, melodies and tunes. Glockenspiel and chime bars, triangles, finger cymbals and metallic percussion

**Release from tension** a fall in pitch. Dissonance resolves to harmony. A drop in volume. Thinning texture

**Relaxation** a moderate, steady tempo, slow-moving chords and arpeggios. Gentle sound sources. Harmonious, steady repetition. Drones and pedal bass

**Sadness** minor keys, dorian mode, minor chords. Slow tempi, sustained notes

**Space** electronic sounds and effects. Long-held notes with open intervals such as 5ths and 7ths e.g. the *Star Trek* interval C-Bb (7th). Explore the general MIDI synth lead, synth pad and synth SFX sounds

**Spooky** the diminished chord (C-Eb-F#-A or D-F-Ab-B). Xylophone sounds, organ sounds. Creaks, ticks and rattles. Portamenti using flute or whistle sounds

**Surprise** sudden chords or rapid glissando. The type of chord will reflect the nature of the surprise

**Suspense** silences of unexpected and varying length. Sustained dissonance on high notes. Semitone clashes and semitone clusters. Sound of ticking, sudden loud moments followed by long quiet periods

**Tension** discords, clashes. Increasing dynamics and tempo. An increasing number of instruments, sound sources which jar and create discomfort in the listener. A rise in pitch, drum rolls, tremolo, thickening texture

**War and conflict** military style drumming. March rhythms. Mounting discords. Spectacular percussion

# Rhythm glossary

## Note values

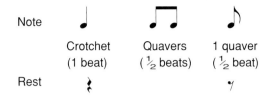

| | | |
|---|---|---|
| Crotchet (1 beat) | Quavers ($\frac{1}{2}$ beats) | 1 quaver ($\frac{1}{2}$ beat) |

Rest

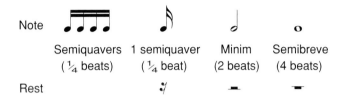

| | | | |
|---|---|---|---|
| Semiquavers ($\frac{1}{4}$ beats) | 1 semiquaver ($\frac{1}{4}$ beat) | Minim (2 beats) | Semibreve (4 beats) |

Rest

## Drum sequencer rhythm grid

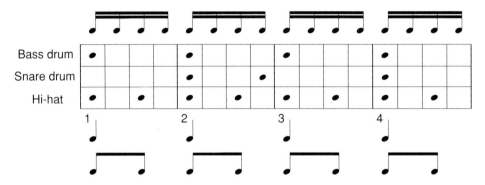

## Time signatures

$\frac{3}{4}$   number of beats per bar   unit (crotchet)    = 3 crotchets per bar

$\frac{6}{8}$   = 6 quavers per bar

## Quantise units

## Some useful rhythmic units in 4/4

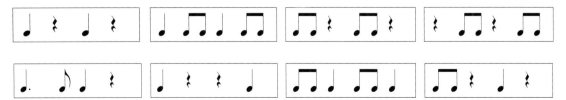

# Pitch glossary

Intervals

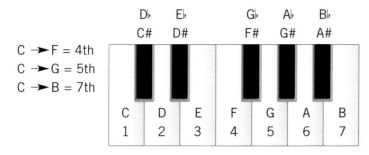

C → F = 4th
C → G = 5th
C → B = 7th

C → C# = semitone
C → D = tone
E → F = semitone
E → F# = tone

# = sharp
♭ = flat

## Major scale in C

## Harmonic minor scale in C

## Key signatures

C Major (A minor)

G major (E minor)
*Uses F#*

D major (B minor)
*Uses F#, C#*

A major (F# minor)
*Uses F#, C#, G#*

F major (D minor)
*Uses B♭*

B♭ major (G minor)
*Uses B♭, E♭*

E♭ major (C minor)
*Uses B♭, E♭, A♭*

## Whole tone scale

(MIDI file 38 has a backing using this scale)

## Chromatic scale

# Chord glossary

### Writing chords down

C = C major     Cm = C minor     $\frac{C}{E}$ = C with E bass     $C^6$ = C with added 6th (A)

### Constructing chords

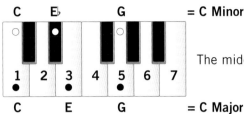

= C Minor

The middle note drops by a semitone to make the chord minor.

= C Major

### Commonly used chords

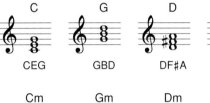

| C | G | D | A | E | B | F | B♭ |
|---|---|---|---|---|---|---|---|
| CEG | GBD | DF♯A | AC♯E | EG♯B | BD♯F♯ | FAC | B♭DF |

| Cm | Gm | Dm | Am | Em | Bm | Fm | B♭m |
|---|---|---|---|---|---|---|---|
| CE♭G | GB♭D | DFA | ACE | EGB | BDF♯ | FA♭C | B♭D♭F |

### Triads (three note chords) in C

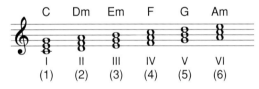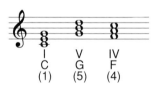

| C | Dm | Em | F | G | Am |
|---|---|---|---|---|---|
| I | II | III | IV | V | VI |
| (1) | (2) | (3) | (4) | (5) | (6) |

| I | V | IV |
|---|---|---|
| C | G | F |
| (1) | (5) | (4) |

### Tonic-dominant-subdominant in eight keys

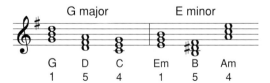

| C major | | | A minor | | |
|---|---|---|---|---|---|
| C | G | F | Am | E | Dm |
| 1 | 5 | 4 | 1 | 5 | 4 |

| G major | | | E minor | | |
|---|---|---|---|---|---|
| G | D | C | Em | B | Am |
| 1 | 5 | 4 | 1 | 5 | 4 |

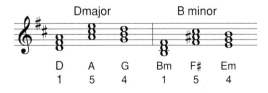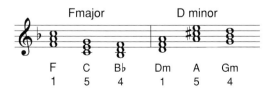

| D major | | | B minor | | |
|---|---|---|---|---|---|
| D | A | G | Bm | F♯ | Em |
| 1 | 5 | 4 | 1 | 5 | 4 |

| F major | | | D minor | | |
|---|---|---|---|---|---|
| F | C | B♭ | Dm | A | Gm |
| 1 | 5 | 4 | 1 | 5 | 4 |

## Inversions

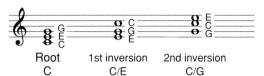

| Root | 1st inversion | 2nd inversion |
|------|---------------|---------------|
| C | C/E | C/G |

## Cadences

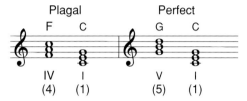

## Suspensions and added notes

# Notation glossary

## Graphic

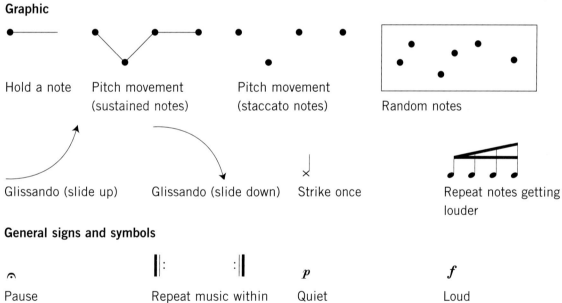

Hold a note    Pitch movement (sustained notes)    Pitch movement (staccato notes)    Random notes

Glissando (slide up)    Glissando (slide down)    Strike once    Repeat notes getting louder

## General signs and symbols

Pause    Repeat music within brackets    *p* Quiet    *f* Loud

Crescendo    Diminuendo    Staccato    Accent

## Standard staff notation

Treble Clef — Middle C: C D E F G A B C D E F G A

Bass Clef: E F G A B C D E F G A B C — Middle C

Note: the direction of the tails changes at the midway point of each staff.

## Notation for chords

C    Cm    $\frac{C}{E}$    $C^6$

## Melody notation using letter names

E G G E D C D E G E D →

## Notation using approximate rhythms

## Notation for melody with chords

## Notation for keyboard instrument

## Notation for three percussion instruments

## Notation for three pitched instruments

## Notation for drum kit

Hi-hat
Snare drum
Bass drum